# Get Your Life

## 7 KEYS TO LIVE A HAPPIER LIFE

CHERYL L THOMAS

Published by:

BE Books
A Division of Becoming Engaged® Enterprises, Inc.
4111 NW 16th Blvd. #358804
Gainesville, Florida 32605

ISBN: 978-0-9797717-1-2

# Acknowledgments

First and foremost, I thank my tribe—my remarkable parents, James and Annie Thomas, and my three amazing sisters, Cassandra, Valerie and Lesley. Your unconditional love and unshakeable belief in my endeavors have been my anchor and my sail. To my extended family, who have cheered me on from the sidelines and celebrated each milestone as their own, thank you for your unwavering encouragement.

I am immensely grateful to my mentors, both near and far, who have generously shared their wisdom, insights, and experiences. Your guidance has not only shaped this book but also sculpted the person I have become.

# Dedication

This book is dedicated to Christian women who are ready to grab hold of the life God designed for your before you were born.

I pray that you know how much God loves you. I pray that you comprehend His desire for you to live a life filled with love, joy, fulfillment in a vibrant community of like-minded people who want you to soar and become everything He desires you to be.

You are not an accident. You are not second rate. You are exceptionally rare and priceless. I pray that truth becomes so ingrained in your mind and being that you accept nothing less than God's bes for you.

May every page in this book remind you that Go is with you, guiding, supporting, and blessing every step you take.

## GET OFF THE SIDELINES OF YOUR LIFE!

For a long time in my life, I lived so far beneath God's will and plan for me. It wasn't because that was what God wanted. It was because I didn't think I deserved it. I thought major blessings only came to "other" people. People who had done more than me. People who sacrificed more. People who lived better. Other people ... not me.

Don't ask me why I thought this way. I wasn't even aware that I did until several years ago. I'd been taught that if God provided a person's basic needs, only greed made them expect more. I was unconsciously pushing abundance away from me with this stinking thinking.

But not anymore. I now know I deserve God's best. It is His will that we all prosper and be in health even as our souls prosper. Not because we've been perfect. Not because we've sacrificed the most or loved the hardest. We deserve it simply because we are His children.

I wrote this book for anyone who has ever thought like I once did. You don't have to live in lack anymore. I am here to sound the alarm so you will know that you truly are deserving of God's absolute best...abundant life. Once you digest this truth, you can have it.

# contents

# contents

# contents

00

00

INTRODUCTION

# A BRIEF NOTE

## Before We
## Begin

When it really comes down to it, true abundance doesn't mean having the most material goods or the fattest bank account. It's not reflected in shopping at the most elite boutiques, dining in the most expensive restaurants nor jet setting to exotic locales. It is finding and fulfilling your God-given purpose with passion and power!

We've got so many questions, but not many answers about life; especially abundant life. People always ask, "What does it mean to live abundantly? What is abundant life and how will I know when I've obtained it?" However, I believe the more important question is,

**Who defines what abundance is for you?"**

What is your formula for life? What many have failed to realize is that no one can create your definition of abundance other than GOD and YOU.

Only you and GOD have the answer to the key to your abundant life. Not me, not your pastor, not the world's greatest talk show or podcast host or your favorite celebrity or guru. Only you. What you must do immediately to begin to live in abundance is to begin answering these questions for yourself.

What will it take for you to feel abundantly happy, blessed and fulfilled? Do you have it now in some measure and don't realize it? Or if not, are you ready to take the necessary steps to create the life you *say* you desire?

If you're not currently satisfied with your life, I have good news. You don't have to stay where you are. You can move from a mundane, boring, unfulfilling life to the purposeful, passionate, exciting life of your dreams. But you have to MAKE it so.

You have to take the necessary steps to take your life from where it is now, to where you want it to be. However, it will only happen when you decide to DO life instead of watching life pass you by.

# WHAT ARE YOU DOING
# WITH YOUR LIFE?

Sometimes we amble through life without purpose and passion. We seem to go wherever the wind blows. Why is that? I believe it's because for the most of us, we've never been taught that our lives are supposed to be lived with purpose and passion.

We've somehow come to believe that all we have to do is just walk through life and wait for life to "happen to us." We've settled into the belief system that says if it is supposed to happen, it will "magically" happen. We've released all of our responsibility to make it so!

Nothing in life is going to magically happen. No one is going to come to your house to offer you a job, a spouse or a better life. Not so. Everything you get out of life will be because you took the time and initiative to make it happen.

You finished high school and college because you got up everyday, went to school, studied and for the most part, passed your tests. You got married because you met someone, spent the necessary time to get to know that person, planned a wedding and life and now work everyday to make it an enjoyable experience.

You got that job because perhaps someone told you about the job opening, you filled out the application, went to the interview and went to work everyday to earn the paycheck you now have the pleasure of receiving.

Everything you now experience is because you were purposeful in obtaining it. Why would we think we wouldn't have to plan for abundance with the same amount of purpose? Abundance doesn't happen because you are a good person.

It doesn't happen just because you are a Christian. It happens because you plan for it and pursue it.

I wrote this book for people who are tired of waiting for abundance to fall into their laps. It is for individuals who have decided to step off the sidelines of their own lives and who are ready to plan and actively pursue the life of their dreams.

This is your life. You should do everything necessary to make sure it is full of the things you enjoy. This book is a jumpstart for your journey. It has in it 7 secrets I believe are necessary to engage in abundant life.

Yes, engage.

According to one definition, in military or police operations, Rules of Engagement (ROE) determine when, where, and how force shall be used. Yes, force. Abundance won't fall into our lap.

We have to dig to find it and work hard to integrate it into our lives. When are you going to get up and get active and involved in plotting the course of your life?

How will you begin to live the abundant life you know God has predestined you to live? What is your strategy? What is your plan of action? What things are paramount to your success? And how will you measure the success you attain?

If we're going to have success in any real measure, we must find the answers to these questions. The answers are locked on the inside of you and this is your invitation to begin the excavation that digs for the treasure in you!

Real success doesn't come easy. It comes with much effort. Be warned, there is no magical formula for success. There will be no one waiting to hand success and abundance to you.

A wise man once said, "Success is intentional." It is not accidental. You don't stumble upon success; you work hard, pray harder and fight your way to abundance. It is the culmination of your efforts.

we want to be successful we will have to confront, ght and overcome destructive habits, fears and the any obstacles that are sure to come. Destiny and urpose won't come easy, but when you uncover lese 7 secrets, you will find yourself headed in the ght direction to fulfillment, purpose and the undant life you crave!

he keys in this book are your strategic plan. They ve you the necessary tools for winning in life. Your st days are ahead of you. Jump in!

# 01

## CHAPTER

### 01

# KEY #1

## *Know*

## YOUR GOD

Do you have a place and time set aside just for you and Jesus? If so, use this time to not only pour out your requests to Him, but to also drink in the richness of His presence. If not, choose a place and time TODAY for a consistent rendezvous with your Savior.

If you're going to depend on God to guide you in your journey, doesn't it just make sense that you should know Him? I'm not talking here about church attendance. I'm not even really talking about your salvation experience. To really know God, you have to spend time with Him. Everyday. Not just when you're in crisis. Not just when you need or want something from Him.

But just as you spend quality and quantity time with those you love when you're seeking to deepen an earthly relationship, you must also spend quality and quantity time with God. Otherwise you're only going to know what other say about Him and not really know Him for yourself.

How often do you pray and what do your prayer consist of? Is it only petition or does it include adoration, praise and thanksgiving?

## DEEPEN YOUR RELATIONSHIP WITH GOD

How often do you meditate on His Word or does your devotion include reading the Bible daily?

God is His Word and if you aren't digesting it daily, you can't know Him in a real, personal way.

Your #1 goal should be to have a relationship with your Savior. You want to know who He is, what He requires of you and why He called and created you. You can only find the answers to these questions by spending ample time with Him everyday.

You want to hear Him whisper why He thinks you're so special and to which group of people your uniqueness was created. You want to know how to take the gifts and talents He's so graciously given you and use them to the best of your ability to accomplish His plan for your life on earth.

Everyone has been given gifts to bless the earth. Most people's gifts lie dormant or severely underutilized because the owner of the gift never consulted the Source of the gift for the application of the gift. Don't allow your gifts and talents to lie dormant. You'll need them to create the life of abundance you seek.

It is through these gifts and talents that God is going to funnel abundance to you. Therefore it is imperative to have a relationship with the only One who can teach you what those gifts are, how you are supposed to use them and how they will bring health and wealth to you and into the earth.

Three Steps to deepen your relationship with God:

- **Step #1: Daily Prayer**
  - This speaks of the time you spend consistently talking with God.

- **Step #2: Daily Meditation**
  - This speaks of the time you spend pondering His conversation with you through His Word.

- **Step #3 Daily Reflection**
  - This speaks of the time you spend asking Him how to make the prayers you prayed and the Word you read relevant in your daily life.

# 02

CHAPTER

# 02

# KEY #2

## YOURSELF

Before you can muster the _courage_ to be yourself, you have to understand who you really are. Beneath all the titles, all the assumptions, and setting aside other people's opinions — do YOU know? You can't reject anyone's perception if you haven't defined or decided who you are. Without God it is impossible to do. Take off all the masks and uncover God's wonder in you.

Before you run full force into your destiny and your life of abundance, you must know who you are. I know it may seem somewhat silly to ask adults, "Who are you?" But the longer I live, the more I realize most people are lost and do not know who they are.

They know who others have said they are, they know clearly the "roles" they play in life, but when you ask the average person who they are, what makes them unique and what their special talents and giftings are, most people stumble.

We often identify ourselves by our roles. So when asked who they are, most people say, "I am an engineer, I am a doctor, I am an entrepreneur, etc." But that doesn't tell me who you are, that tells me what you do. Some even respond, "I am a spouse, parent or friend." That only tells me who you are responsible for and to and not who you are.

Even going further some say, "I am an introvert, extrovert or sensing person." That describes your personality, not what I call your "is-ness." Your "is-ness" is who you are without any outside influences, attachments or identifiers. Without being attached to any other role, what defines you as an individual?

Having trouble? I thought you might. You see, without God's help it's impossible to know. You can't determine the identity of the creation without the creator. So when you're looking to understand who you are, what your unique destiny is and the problem you're predetermined to solve in the earth, you must go to God for the answers.

You can't ask anyone else, because often others will tell you how to become more like them. It's a vicious cycle. We attempt to find a "pattern" that already exists in the earth and teach others to mimic or model those persons.

# DARE TO BE DIFFERENT

We are not trained to be different. The world we live in encourages us to all be the same. It's the false idea of conformity that keeps many bound in a life of monotony. If we were all supposed to walk alike, talk alike or think alike what a drab world this would be. The thing that makes life exciting and spontaneity so divine is the beauty in our differences.

Now, while it may be smart to model and mimic processes, it is never wise to model or mimic another person's "is-ness." If you do this you're robbing the world of the incredible unique gift that is you. Without the gift of you the world won't have access to what we need to prosper and flourish.

So, what is your uniqueness? What sets you apart from all others? What gift do you have to offer the world that no one else can offer quite the way you can offer?

To assist you on your journey to you, I've included some questions that will help you narrow your focus and hopefully shorten the journey to finding the answers you need to start living in abundance. Really reflect and prayerfully seek God for the answers to these questions as they hold the key to unlocking your life of abundance.

**Questions:**

What are your dreams?

What do you do without fear?

What are you great at?

What motivates you?

What interests you?
What makes you happy? Sad? Mad?

What energizes you?

What makes you feel rested? Relaxed? Renewed?

What would you do if you knew you couldn't fail?
What would you do for free? (If all other needs were met)

What makes you feel fulfilled?

What brings you complete joy?

When was the last time you felt fulfilled?
What was that like? What were you doing?

What are the gifts that God has placed in your heart?

Are there gifts and abilities that He's given to you that have been buried deep inside?

To really "know" yourself, you have to dig deep. You have to look beyond the mere surface and the superficial things most people notice. Transfix on your own reflection in the mirror and ask yourself who you are. Set aside what other people say or have said. This is not about the opinions of others. This is your survey. What is unique about you? Is it your sense of humor, your unique style, your giving spirit or infectious zest for love and life? What do you have to offer the world that no other person can? This is a divine appointment to be self-absorbed. Educate yourself about who you are.

CHAPTER

# KEY #3

## YOUR PURPOSE

What sets you apart? What do you do easily that others struggle to do?

What do you love? What brings you "pure" joy?

As you answer these questions, look deep within yourself to see the treasure God has placed within you.

What are you uniquely gifted to do? What do you do well without much effort? What problem in the earth brings you the most angst, disappointment?

When you're trying to determine your <u>purpose</u>, the question you're really trying to answer is not only what I am here to do, but why am I here? Why is my presence necessary?

You see, one of the reasons you're on the earth is to solve a problem. Your agenda is to find out what that problem is and to find innovative and creative ways to solve it.

That's why when you're trying to find the key to your purpose, you also look for problems that pain you. Because it takes a strong passion and pull to fulfill purpose. The problem you're to solve will have to hurt you enough for you to come out of your comfort zone and risk the pain and rejection you may encounter in your journey to solve the problem.

You have to be <u>passionate</u> about its solution, so you have to have the heart, courage and strength to see it through.

So look for issues that in society, your community and the world that make you want to make a definite difference because these are clues that are meant to lead you to your purpose.

## BE A CHANGE AGENT

When you find those issues, check you
past to see why these particular issues
grieve you. Is it an issue you too have
encountered or by which you've been
encumbered?

Many times this is the case, which is
why you've been called to address it.

You need to be acquainted with the problem to administer the help and assistance necessary and to identify with those who may currently be going through the trauma you have now escaped.

But don't stop at discovering your purpose. It does no one any good for you to know your purpose and not do anything to fulfill it. Once you're aware of what you were born to do, you must boldly begin the journey to walk it out. This takes courage beyond belief. Everyone may not agree with you.

Everyone won't help you. And some may even discourage you. But once God has illuminated your purpose to you, you must do everything you can to fulfill it. He chose you because He knew you had the skills, the tools and the compassion to complete this assignment.

He is counting on you to push past the naysayers, the doubters and to run toward your purpose with passion, determination and excitement. You were born to do this. And with God's help, you can do this.

Do it now!

04

CHAPTER

04

# KEY #4

## *Know*

# YOUR FUN

With all the stress life hurls at us on a daily basis, we must find a way to relax, recharge and usher our minds to a place of fun & frivolity.

Laughter is one of the best ways to pierce the clouds of anxiety and worry. It's free and it's fun so go ahead and laugh it out now.

Fun. There I said it. It seems to be the "dirty" little word in many Christian circles. We'll gladly spend hours in shut-in services, the next revival, conference or seminar of epic proportion, but somehow when you mention the word fun in a Christian setting it's almost sacrilege.

Then we wonder why we can't win the world for Christ. Maybe it's because some Christians come off like mean, angry people who despise or forbid any activity that bears any remote resemblance to fun. Maybe the world looks at our lives and sees only rules, regulations and guidelines.

Why are we so afraid to have fun? Why is getting some Christians to engage in fun activities almost as difficult as pulling teeth? Do we think fun is sinful?

Do we think that anyone who would dare indulge in any fun activity would somehow lose their salvation?

Jesus said that He came that we might have life and have it more abundantly. He came to give us abundance in LIFE. His Word also tells us that He giveth to us richly all things to ENJOY.

You can have fun. *Pure* fun. It's healthy and a proven stress reliever. The world seems to have a monopoly on fun. Let's show the world that they really haven't experienced real fun until they've experienced fun as a Christian. No hangovers, no memory losses and no regrets. This is fun that you can actually talk about with your children and not be embarrassed or ashamed. Pure, clean and incredible, mind-renewing, heartwarming fun.

# IT'S OK TO BE HAPPY!

When was the last time you had one of those gut-busting, side-splitting laughs? You know the kind that just feels good, like a breath of fresh air. It's therapeutic. If you haven't had one in a while, that means you're either stressed, overworked or have become numb to life. Relax. It's time for you to live. Laughter is one of th richest rewards in life.

t cleanses your spirit and fills your soul. The Bible ys a merry heart doeth good like a medicine. When as the last time you took your "medicine?" It's eat medicine that we should all take daily.

on't be afraid. It's really okay to let the kid in you rface. It's okay to lay down all of your "adult" ties and responsibilities to breathe, relax and be sponsible for nothing else but creating a fun vironment for yourself.

u'll be surprised at how energized and alive you l. Engaging in creative activities awakens your rit to the boundless opportunities all around you.

But I must warn you ... having fun is addictive. Once you begin a regular diet of fun, you won't ever want to stop. You'll wonder why it took you so long to truly live and enjoy life. It is also very contagious. Fun people are like magnets. They always draw others. Everyone wants to be around someone who brings light and laughter into a room.

You've witnessed that person walking into a somber party and their infectious attitude lit up the entire room. Deep down inside, did you ever envy that person? You don't have to be jealous anymore, by developing a life of love and fun, you will BE that person.

That person is on the inside of you screaming to get out. Find the courage to free them. Take the time to find the beauty in today and everyday. Whether it is a rainy day, sunny day, or a snowy day it is a good day.

God places incredible beauty all around us waiting for us to notice it, cherish it and celebrate it. Don't disappoint Him by being too overwhelmed by your overloaded schedule to see it. Stop. Take a deep breath. Take off your work hat. It's time to play!

# 05

## CHAPTER

# 05

# KEY #5

## WHEN TO REST

You are no good to yourself or
to anyone else tired and worn
out. You miss the best of you
and the world misses the best
of you.

Take the necessary time to
recharge, refresh and renew.
We need you at your best!

How do you spell relief? How and when do you rest? According to Merriam Webster's Dictionary, the definition of rest is freedom from activity or labor, a state of motionlessness or inactivity. Another definition states it is peace of mind or spirit and freedom from anxiety.

Rest in the verb tense means to cease from action or motion, to refrain from labor or exertion. But the best definition means to remain confident (trust).

However, no matter how eloquent or descriptive, most people already know the "definition" of rest They just don't do it.

No matter how many neurologists, psychologists or biologists confirm the medical benefits of rest or the dire consequences that could impair our physical bodies because of the lack of rest, we somehow seem to turn a deaf ear to the cold hard truth.

Our bodies need rest. Our minds need rest. Our spirit and soul needs rest. It is not even an option. Either you rest voluntarily or your body will shut down and make you rest. Why put yourself and your family and friends through that kind of unnecessary stress and trauma?

Rest. Now. Right Now. The world is not going to collapse if you don't rest, but you might if you don't know when to say when.

## CHILL OUT!

Resting doesn't only mean "inaction," i is a confident trust that your heavenly Father has everything under control. A much as our action doesn't affirm it, God, the Creator and Mastermind of th entire universe, does know what He is doing.

He truly doesn't need our assistance to make the world go around.

It was functioning perfectly before we got here and will continue to function long after we're gone. We have to learn how to trust God enough to let go and trust Him with our lives.

My word for you today is - REST. You don't have to know the next move. God does. As long as He does, victory is always sure. Sooo..... Rest. God's got this!

Breathe in the beauty of each new day. Enjoy the innocent laughter of a child; bathe in the wisdom of your elders. Take the day off from being an adult.

Shake off the inhibitions adulthood inevitably brings. Today you are simply God's child. Enjoy it!

# 06

CHAPTER

06

# KEY # 6

*Know*

## YOUR TRIBE

Who speaks into your life?
Who are your mentors or
<u>coaches</u>?

Do you have any or are you
attempting to face life by
yourself?

Who has God called to walk with you through your journey? Who speaks into your life when you're facing trials and tragedy? Who speaks encouragement to lift you when you're down?

If you're going to have great victory, you'll need great mentors and <u>coaches</u>. These are the people God has called to encourage, equip and help you plot your course. They're advisors who have been where you are now seeking to go.

You'll need their advice, wisdom and even sometimes their correction as you go. The Bible says that in the multitude of counselors, there is safety. They are your safety net. They tell you which pitfalls to be aware of, which shortcuts to take and how to make sure your life is in balance.

On your journey take time to listen to God's promptings when He brings them into your life. Know who they are. If you want to be successful in your journey, you'll have to be sensitive to the voice of God and be listening for His direction. He'll show you who to trust, who is in your corner and those who are not.

Never negate His instructions. Never second guess His wisdom. After all, He did create the world. He knows exactly who to assign to your journey.

You'll also need to keep your family and friends close. No matter how life batters you, they are your constant companions and they cheer you on and offer you the much needed love and support that will sustain you when you want to give up.

# FIND YOUR COMMUNITY!

*Now really look at the beauty of your spouse, your children, your family and friends. They are precious gifts to you. When was the last time you had fun with them?*

*Don't let another day go by without enjoying seeing their smiling faces and appreciating the blessing they are to you.*

They are your safe place. The place you can go when you're discouraged. The place you find refuge when you're afraid. The place you find serenity when you're overwhelmed. The place where you can take your superhero cape off and just be yourself. They love you unconditionally and allow you to rest and refresh without judgment, without agenda and without needing you to perform. They let you be you.

Know the difference between your mentors and your friends. While your mentors can be your friends, that is not their assignment. Their assignment is to get you running diligently toward your purpose and goal. They might not offer you the warm fuzzy you seek from family and friends because they know what God has called them to do. And that is to steer you in the path of your destiny, not placate you.

But to be successful and balanced, you need both. <u>Mentors</u> to challenge you and family and friends to comfort you. Mentors to stretch you and family to massage you when you're weary.

Your journey will be challenging, but it will be worth every struggle, every tear and every sacrifice you make to be the best you God has destined you to be. Keep your tribe close. You'll need them in the days, weeks and years to come.

# 07

## CHAPTER

# 07

# KEY #7

## LIVE
## AUTHENTICALLY

Whose playbook are you living by? Yours or the playbook of your friends? You'll never experience abundant life trying to walk out someone else's journey. You must find courage to blaze your own trail, make your own mistakes or missteps, but ultimately find the path that leads to a contented life.... For you! Not the life your parents always wanted, the life your friends enjoy, but the life that is tailor made precisely for you alone.

The road to greatness is not an easy one. If it were, more people would travel it. It is one wrought with difficulty, sacrifice and constantly strips you out of complacency. It is for the fearless few who sense the urging to be and do more and have the discipline to continue the journey no matter how difficult the struggle.

The prize ahead is so great and magnificent, they are willing to endure momentary affliction to enjoy the benefits and reward of reaching their maximum potential. While some settle for average, they will not stop until they are excellent. They have an inner innate drive to stretch their abilities and capabilities until they see in the physical what God has shown them in their spirits.

Are you one of these people? Do you hunger to identify, cultivate and develop the greatness on the inside of you? If so, your journey begins now. You are unique and divine. There is no one on the face of the Earth quite like you.

No one can do what you are called to do like you can do it. The world is awaiting the genius in you. Take the time to uncover it, nurture and develop it, but most importantly share it with the world. Please don't disappoint us. We're waiting on you!

08

FINAL
WORDS

08

# BONUS KEY #8

*Final*

# WORDS

I'm excited about your journey to your purpose. Some are just beginning the trek, while others are well on their way. Wherever you are in your journey, I just want you to know that it is closer than being within your grasp, it's in your mind. As soon as you believe it can be so, it will. You're not waiting for it to happen to you, it is as close as your next thought coupled with the necessary action to fulfill it.

One year from now, would you like for your life to be 3 times better? Would you like to be walking in your purpose and living the life you love? To help you get started on this journey, I've opened a community of women of faith 40+ years young dedicated to the art living happier lives.

Click the link on the next page and get ready to begin your journey to PurposeFULL YOU!

JOIN The BE Club

# INNER
# CIRCLE

Helping Women of Faith Lead Happier Lives

www.CherylThomas.co/TBCICP

WHERE PERSONAL
DEVELOPMENT MEETS FUN!

# A few Books by Cheryl

Need a faith boost? In this 52-Week Prayer and Affirmation Journal, discover how to trust God again and how to BELIEVE God to fulfill every promise He's spoken over your life!

Finally, a book for every person of faith who has lived the bulk of life spinning on the exhausting wheel of trying to live up to other people's expectations. This powerful book reveals the much needed exit ramp off that hellacious emotional roller coaster and offers the respite of a cruise on the ship of God's acceptance and unwavering approval of you as His child.

## Cheryl THomas

CherylThomasSpeaks@gmail.com
www.CherylThomas.co
@CherylThomasSpeaks

It is Cheryl's joy to speak life, hope and encouragement into people's lives. She sees it as her mission to inspire, challenge and light the fire in Christian women to produce the life God is calling for them to live.

Cheryl is often invited to speak at Church, Community, Women's, Youth, Singles and Inspirational/Motivational events. To secure Cheryl for a seminar, workshop or to be a speaker at your next conference, retreat or seminar, please feel free to email her office at admin@CherylThomas.co.

Made in United States
Orlando, FL
27 November 2024

54064779R10055